Welcome go to Romania: 2023 Detailed Travel Guide to Romania, for Visitors and Tourists.

By: Henry Miles

Copyright

Table of contents

Introduction to Romanian life for Visitors and Tourists

Welcome to Romania, a country full of history, culture, and natural beauty! Located in the heart of Europe, Romania is a land of contrasts, where ancient traditions and modern lifestyles blend in perfect harmony.

As a tourist, you'll find a wealth of things to see and do here. From the majestic Carpathian Mountains to the stunning Black Sea coast, Romania has something for everyone. Explore medieval castles and fortresses, sample delicious cuisine, and immerse yourself in the vibrant cultural scene.

Romania is also a country of friendly and hospitable people who take pride in sharing their traditions and way of life with visitors. Whether you're strolling through the charming streets of Bucharest, attending a folk festival, or visiting a rural village, you'll find that Romania is a place where the warmth of the people is as inspiring as the beauty of the landscape.

So come and discover Romania for yourself! Whether you're here for a short visit or a longer stay, you'll find that this country has a lot to offer and will leave you with unforgettable memories.

The daily activities in Romania from Monday to Sunday, for visitors

Here's a sample itinerary of daily activities that visitors can enjoy in Romania from Monday to Sunday:

Monday: Start the week by exploring the vibrant city of Bucharest. Visit the Palace of the Parliament, the second-largest administrative building in the world, and take a stroll in the charming old town. Have lunch at a traditional Romanian restaurant and try local specialties like sarmale (stuffed cabbage rolls) or mici (grilled minced meat rolls).

Tuesday: Venture out of the city and head to the famous Peles Castle in Sinaia, a stunning royal residence nestled in the Carpathian Mountains. Take a guided tour of the castle and its grounds, and enjoy the breathtaking views of the surrounding forests.

Wednesday: Visit the painted monasteries of Bucovina, a UNESCO World Heritage Site known for its unique frescoes and colorful decorations. Explore the Voronet Monastery, also known as the "Sistine Chapel of the East," and learn about the fascinating history of these religious buildings.

Thursday: Discover the traditional villages of Maramures, where time seems to have stood still. Visit the wooden churches, explore the local markets, and learn about the customs and traditions of this rural region. Don't miss the chance to try some homemade plum brandy, a local specialty.

Friday: Take a break and relax on the Black Sea coast. Visit the lively resort town of Mamaia, known for its sandy beaches and vibrant nightlife. Enjoy a swim in the sea, sunbathe on the beach, and sample some fresh seafood at one of the many restaurants.

Saturday: Go hiking in the breathtaking Fagaras Mountains, the highest peaks in Romania. Take a guided trek to the summit of Moldoveanu Peak, the highest point in the country, and enjoy the stunning views of the surrounding valleys and forests.

Sunday: Visit the picturesque town of Sighisoara, a UNESCO World Heritage Site and the birthplace of Vlad the Impaler, the inspiration for the legend of Dracula. Explore the medieval citadel, visit the Clock Tower Museum, and enjoy the local cuisine at one of the charming restaurants.

Romanian Language

The Romanian language is a Romance language spoken by approximately 24 million people, primarily in Romania and Moldova. It is also spoken by Romanian communities in other countries, such as Italy, Spain, Germany, and the United States.

The Romanian language uses the Latin alphabet, and its grammar and vocabulary are derived primarily from Latin, with influences from Slavic, Greek, and Turkish.

Here are some common Romanian phrases and their English meanings:

Bună dimineața - Good morning

Cum te numesti? (What is your name?)

Ma numesc... (My name is...)

Bine ați venit - Welcome

Ce mai faci? - How are you?

Mulțumesc - Thank you

Cu plăcere - You're welcome

La revedere - Goodbye

Te iubesc - I love you

Îmi pare rău - I'm sorry

Unde este toaleta? - Where is the bathroom?

Cât costă? - How much does it cost?

The Fagaras Mountain in Romania.

Accommodations in Romania

Romania is a beautiful and diverse country with a rich history and culture, attracting many visitors and tourists every year. There are many accommodations in Romania that cater to various budgets and preferences, ranging from luxurious hotels to cozy guesthouses and affordable hostels.

Hotels are the most common type of accommodation in Romania, especially in major cities such as Bucharest, Cluj-Napoca, and Timisoara. There are many international hotel chains as well as local ones, offering a wide range of facilities and services, such as swimming pools, fitness centers, restaurants, and conference rooms. Prices for hotels in Romania vary depending on the location, season, and quality, but generally, they are affordable compared to Western Europe.

If you are looking for a more authentic experience, you can stay in guesthouses or bed and breakfasts, which are scattered throughout the country, especially in rural areas. Guesthouses are usually family-owned and operated, providing guests with a warm and friendly atmosphere. They offer comfortable rooms with private or shared bathrooms, and sometimes, home-cooked meals made with locally sourced ingredients. Guesthouses in Romania are a great way to get to know the local culture and traditions and are often located in picturesque settings, such as in the mountains or near historic landmarks.

For budget-conscious travelers, hostels are a popular option in Romania, particularly in larger cities. Hostels offer dormitory-style accommodation with shared bathrooms and communal spaces, such as kitchens and lounges. They are an excellent choice for solo travelers or groups of friends who want to meet new people and save money on accommodation. Hostels in Romania are generally clean and safe, and many offer additional services, such as tours, bike rentals, and social events.

If you prefer more independent accommodation, you can rent apartments or villas in Romania, especially for longer stays. There are many websites and platforms that offer short-term rentals in Romania, allowing you to live like a local and explore the country at your own pace. Renting an apartment or villa can be a great option if you are traveling with family or friends and want more space and privacy.

Accommodation Prices in Romania: to help you make your budget as a visitor.

The price of accommodations in Romania can vary widely depending on several factors, such as the location, type of accommodation, and time of year.

In general, budget accommodation options such as hostels and guesthouses can cost between 25-60 RON (5-12 USD) per night for a dorm bed, while private rooms can range from 70-200 RON (15-45 USD) per night. Mid-range hotels and apartments can cost between 200-500 RON (45-110 USD) per night, while luxury hotels and resorts can range from 500-1500 RON (110-330 USD) per night or even more.

Prices can be higher in popular tourist destinations such as Bucharest, Brasov, and the Black Sea coast, especially during peak season (June-August). It's also worth noting that prices may fluctuate based on events, festivals, and other special occasions.

Romania offers a wide range of accommodations for visitors and tourists, catering to various budgets and preferences. Whether you are looking for a luxurious hotel, a cozy guesthouse, an affordable hostel, or an independent apartment or villa, you are sure to find something that suits your needs and tastes.

Food and drink you can never say no to in Romania

Romanian cuisine is a blend of Eastern European and Balkan flavors, influenced by the country's long history and varied geography. Traditional Romanian dishes feature hearty stews, grilled meats, and flavorful soups, often accompanied by pickled vegetables and bread.

One of the most famous Romanian dishes is sarmale, which are stuffed cabbage rolls filled with a mixture of ground pork, rice, and spices. Another popular dish is mici, which are small grilled rolls of minced meat seasoned with garlic and paprika. Other notable meat dishes include tocana, a stew made with beef or pork, and papanasi, a dessert of fried cheese dumplings served with sour cream and jam.

Romanian cuisine also features a wide range of soups, including ciorba, a sour soup made with meat or vegetables and flavored with dill, and zacusca, a vegetable spread made from roasted eggplant and peppers.

When it comes to drinks, Romania is known for its wine and brandy production. Some of the most popular Romanian wines include Feteasca Neagra and Feteasca Alba, which are both made from local grape varieties. Palinka, a traditional fruit brandy, is also a popular drink in Romania and is typically made from plums or other fruits.

In addition to wine and brandy, Romania is also known for its beer production. Some of the most popular Romanian beers include Ursus and Timisoreana, both of which are lagers.

Romanian cuisine offers a diverse range of flavors and textures, with a focus on hearty, filling dishes and traditional ingredients. Whether you're looking for meaty stews or fresh, flavorful soups, Romania has something to offer for every palate.

Don't get confused on where to get some good foods and drinks while in Romania

Romania has a diverse culinary scene with a mix of traditional and modern restaurants. Here are some of the famous eateries in Romania:

Caru' cu bere - Located in the heart of Bucharest, Caru' cu bere is a historic restaurant that dates back to 1879. It's known for its traditional Romanian dishes, including sarmale and mici, and its stunning architecture.

Hanul lui Manuc - Another historic restaurant in Bucharest, Hanul lui Manuc was established in 1808 and is one of the oldest in the city. It serves traditional Romanian cuisine in a traditional setting, with a large courtyard and a spacious indoor dining area.

Lacrimi si Sfinti - This modern restaurant in Bucharest is known for its innovative takes on traditional Romanian dishes. The menu changes seasonally and features fresh, locally-sourced ingredients.

La Mama - With multiple locations throughout Romania, La Mama is a popular restaurant chain that serves traditional Romanian cuisine in a casual setting. The menu includes a range of soups, stews, and grilled meats.

Beraria H - Located in the historic Cotroceni neighborhood of Bucharest, Beraria H is a popular beer garden that serves a range of local and international beers, as well as traditional Romanian dishes like mici and tocana.

Casa Bunicii 2 - This family-owned restaurant in Brasov serves traditional Romanian dishes in a cozy, home-like setting. The menu includes soups, stews, and grilled meats, as well as homemade desserts.

These are just a few examples of the many restaurants and eateries in Romania that offer delicious food and a unique dining experience.

Attractions in Romania

Romania is a beautiful and fascinating country located in Southeastern Europe, known for its stunning landscapes, rich cultural heritage, and vibrant cities. From the picturesque villages of Transylvania to the majestic Carpathian Mountains and the vibrant capital city of Bucharest, Romania has much to offer for tourists seeking a unique and memorable experience.

Here are some of the top attractions to visit in Romania:

Bran Castle - Also known as "Dracula's Castle," this Gothic fortress is located in the heart of Transylvania and is one of Romania's most famous landmarks. It is said to have inspired Bram Stoker's Dracula novel and is now a popular tourist destination. Below is the picture of Bran Castle in Romania.

Peles Castle - Located in the mountain resort town of Sinaia, this beautiful castle was once the summer residence of the Romanian royal family.

It features stunning architecture and is surrounded by beautiful gardens and forests.

Transfagarasan Highway - This scenic road winds through the Carpathian Mountains and offers breathtaking views of the surrounding landscape. It is considered one of the most beautiful and challenging drives in the world.

Painted Monasteries of Bucovina - These UNESCO World Heritage sites are located in northeastern Romania and are famous for their colorful frescoes and beautiful architecture. They are a must-visit for anyone interested in Byzantine art and Orthodox spirituality.

The Danube Delta - This unique wetland area is the second-largest river delta in Europe and is home to a rich variety of flora and fauna. It is a paradise for birdwatchers and nature lovers and offers a peaceful escape from the hustle and bustle of the city.

Bucharest - Romania's capital city is a vibrant and dynamic metropolis that combines traditional architecture with modern amenities. It features numerous museums, art galleries, restaurants, and nightlife spots, making it a popular destination for tourists from all over the world.

Sighisoara - This medieval fortified city is located in Transylvania and is one of the best-preserved examples of a medieval citadel in Europe. It features narrow cobblestone streets, colorful houses, and a beautiful clock tower that offers stunning views of the surrounding countryside.

These are just a few of the many attractions that Romania has to offer. Whether you are interested in history, culture, nature, or adventure, you are sure to find something that appeals to you in this beautiful and diverse country.

How to make the best of these attractive places in Romania

Romania has many attractive places to visit, and visitors and tourists can make the best out of their trip by following these tips:

Explore the capital city of Bucharest: Bucharest is a vibrant and lively city with a rich history, culture, and architecture. Visitors can take a walk around the old town, visit the Palace of the Parliament, the largest administrative building in the world, and the Romanian

Athenaeum, a concert hall and a landmark of the city.

Discover the beauty of Transylvania: Transylvania is a region in Romania with a rich history, culture, and stunning natural landscapes. Visitors can explore the fortified Saxon villages of Sighisoara, Brasov, and Sibiu, which are UNESCO World Heritage sites. They can also visit the famous Bran Castle, which is associated with the legend of Dracula.

Visit the Painted Monasteries of Bucovina: The Painted Monasteries of Bucovina are a group of eight Eastern Orthodox monasteries, famous for their unique frescoes painted on the exterior walls. The monasteries are included in UNESCO's World Heritage List and are a must-see for any visitor to Romania.

Enjoy the stunning nature: Romania has many natural wonders to explore, including the Danube Delta, the Carpathian Mountains, and the Black Sea coast. Visitors can go hiking, skiing, or enjoy water sports, such as rafting and kayaking.

Taste the local cuisine: Romanian cuisine is delicious and diverse, with influences from Turkish, Greek, and Hungarian cuisines. Visitors can try traditional dishes such as sarmale, mici, and ciorba, and taste local wines and spirits, such as tuica and palinca.

Attend traditional festivals and events: Romania has many traditional festivals and events, such as the Merry Cemetery in Maramures, the Bear Festival in Brasov, and the

Wine Festival in Bucharest. These events provide an opportunity to experience the local culture and traditions.

Engage with the locals: Romanians are friendly and welcoming, and visitors can learn a lot about the local culture and way of life by engaging with the locals. Visitors can participate in workshops, such as traditional handicrafts or cooking classes, or attend local events and festivals.

The Medieval Castle in Romania.

Transportation in Romania

Romania has a relatively developed transportation network that includes various modes of transportation such as roads, railways, airports, and waterways. Here's an overview of the transportation network in Romania:

Roads: Romania has a road network of over 86,000 kilometers, of which approximately 46,000 kilometers are paved. The major highways in Romania include the A1, A2, A3, A4, A6, A10, and A11. The A1 highway, also known as the Sun Highway, is the most important highway in Romania and connects Bucharest with the western part of the country. Romania also has an extensive network of national and county roads that provide connectivity to various parts of the country.

Railways: Romania has a rail network of approximately 10,500 kilometers, of which around 70% are electrified. The railway system in Romania is operated by CFR (Căile Ferate Române) and connects major cities and towns across the country. The most important railway line is the Bucharest-Brasov-Cluj-Napoca-Oradea line, which runs from the capital to the western border of the country.

Airports: Romania has 17 airports, out of which four are international airports - Bucharest Henri Coanda International Airport, Cluj-Napoca International Airport, Timisoara Traian Vuia International Airport, and Iasi International

Airport. These airports handle a significant amount of air traffic and connect Romania to various destinations across Europe and beyond.

Waterways: Romania has a network of rivers and canals that provide access to the Black Sea and the Danube River. The most important river ports are located in Galati, Braila, and Constanta. The port of Constanta is the largest port in Romania and handles a significant amount of cargo traffic.

Overall, the transportation network in Romania is well-developed and provides good connectivity within the country and to neighboring countries. However, there are still some challenges, such as inadequate funding for infrastructure development and maintenance, which need to be addressed to further improve the transportation network in Romania.

Transportation budget in Romania

The cost of transportation in Romania varies depending on the mode of transportation and the distance traveled.

Public transportation in Romania is generally affordable, with the cost of a one-way ticket for a bus, tram, or metro ride in major cities ranging from 1.5 RON (approximately 0.3 USD) to 3 RON (approximately 0.6 USD), depending on the city and the length of the journey. Monthly passes are also available and can be a cost-effective option for frequent travelers.

Taxis are also widely available in Romania and are generally affordable compared to other European countries. The initial fare for a taxi ride is around 2.5 RON (approximately 0.5 USD), and the price per kilometer ranges from 1.79 RON (approximately 0.36 USD) to 3 RON (approximately 0.6 USD), depending on the city and the taxi company.

If you prefer to rent a car, the cost varies depending on the car model and rental period. Generally, car rental companies in Romania offer daily rates ranging from 100 RON (approximately 20 USD) to 400 RON (approximately 80 USD) per day for a standard car, depending on the season and the length of the rental period.

It is worth noting that Romania has a relatively extensive railway network, and train travel can be an affordable and convenient way to get around the country. The cost of a train ticket varies depending on the distance traveled, the type of train, and the class of travel. For example, a one-way ticket for a local train ride between two nearby cities can cost around 10-20 RON (approximately 2-4 USD), while a long-distance trip on an express train can cost between 50-100 RON (approximately 10-20 USD).

The cost of transportation in Romania is generally affordable and varies depending on the mode of transportation, the distance traveled, and the season.

Shopping in Romania

Romania has a diverse and dynamic shopping scene, with a range of options from traditional outdoor markets to modern malls. If you're looking for a shopping experience in Romania, here's what you can expect:

Obor Market in Bucharest

Outdoor Markets: One of the most popular and traditional ways of shopping in Romania is to visit an outdoor market. These markets offer a range of goods such as fresh produce, clothing, souvenirs, and household items. Some of the most popular markets in Romania include the Obor Market in Bucharest, the Piata Centrala in Cluj-Napoca, and the Piata Unirii in Iasi.

Shopping Malls: Romania has many modern shopping malls that offer a wide range of stores, from international brands to local boutiques. Some of the most popular malls in Romania include AFI Cotroceni in Bucharest, Iulius Mall in Cluj-Napoca, and Baneasa Shopping City in Bucharest.

Traditional Crafts: Romania is known for its traditional crafts such as pottery, woodcarving, and embroidery. You can find these crafts in local markets and stores, particularly in rural areas.

Souvenirs: Romania has many souvenirs to choose from, including traditional clothing, pottery, and wooden toys. You can find these items in markets and souvenir shops throughout the country.

Supermarkets: For day-to-day shopping needs, there are many supermarkets in Romania, including Carrefour, Auchan, and Mega Image. These supermarkets offer a wide range of goods at affordable prices.

Online Shopping: Online shopping is becoming increasingly popular in Romania, with many international retailers such as Amazon and Zara offering online shopping options. There are also many Romanian-based online retailers such as eMag and Altex.

In terms of prices, Romania can be quite affordable for shopping, particularly in comparison to other European countries. However, prices can vary depending on the location and type of store. In general, outdoor markets and traditional crafts tend to be more affordable, while shopping malls and international retailers may be more expensive.

Shopping in Romania offers a diverse range of options, from traditional outdoor markets to modern malls. Whether you're looking for souvenirs, traditional crafts, or everyday goods, you're sure to find something that suits your needs and budget.

Culture and Customs in Romania: all you need to know

The Romanians are a diverse ethnic group with a rich culture and unique customs. They are a Latin-based people with a complex history, having been influenced by various cultures and civilizations throughout their history. Here are some of the main aspects of Romanian culture and customs:

Language: The Romanian language is a Romance language that evolved from Latin. It is the official language of Romania and Moldova, and is also spoken in parts of Ukraine, Serbia, and Hungary. The language has evolved over time and has been influenced by other languages such as Turkish, Slavic, and Hungarian.

Religion: The majority of Romanians are Eastern Orthodox Christians, but there are also Catholic, Protestant, and Jewish minorities. Religion plays an important role in Romanian culture, and religious holidays such as Christmas and Easter are widely celebrated.

Folk traditions: Romanian folklore includes a rich mix of songs, dances, and stories. Folk costumes are also an important part of Romanian culture, with each region having its own unique style of dress. Traditional handicrafts, such as pottery, woodcarving, and embroidery, are also an important part of Romanian folk culture.

Cuisine: Romanian cuisine is a mix of influences from the Balkans, Austria, and Turkey. Popular dishes include sarmale (stuffed cabbage rolls), mici (grilled minced meat rolls), and mamaliga (cornmeal porridge). Romanian wines are also gaining recognition on the international stage.

Celebrations and festivals: Romanians love to celebrate, and there are numerous festivals and holidays throughout the year. One of the most famous is Dracula's Castle Party, held annually in Bran Castle. Other popular festivals include the Sighisoara Medieval Festival, the Transilvania International Film Festival, and the Romanian Traditional Craftsmen's Fair.

Etiquette and customs: Romanians are generally warm and friendly people, but they also value politeness and respect. Greetings are important, with handshakes being the most common form of greeting between strangers.

When visiting someone's home, it is customary to bring a small gift such as flowers or chocolates. It is also important to dress neatly and conservatively, especially when visiting churches or other religious sites.

Romanian culture is a fascinating blend of traditions, history, and influences from neighboring cultures. The country's diverse customs, cuisine, and festivals make it an exciting and unique destination for travelers.

The Sighisoara Medieval festival of the Romanians

The Sighisoara Medieval Festival is an annual event held in the town of Sighisoara, Romania. This festival celebrates the medieval history of the region and attracts visitors from all over the world. Here is more information about this unique and exciting event:

History: The festival was first held in 1992, and has since become one of the most popular cultural events in Romania. The festival is held in the old citadel of Sighisoara, which is a UNESCO World Heritage Site. The town itself dates back to the 12th century and is known for its well-preserved medieval architecture.

Activities: During the festival, visitors can enjoy a wide range of activities and events. These include live performances, medieval games and competitions, traditional crafts and artisanal demonstrations, food and drink stalls, and much more. The festival culminates with a grand parade through the town, featuring participants dressed in medieval costumes and carrying banners and flags.

Medieval reenactments: One of the highlights of the festival is the medieval reenactments. Visitors can witness demonstrations of medieval combat and watch knights jousting on horseback. Other reenactments include archery contests, traditional dances, and musical performances.

Costumes: Visitors are encouraged to dress up in medieval attire, which adds to the festive atmosphere of the event. Many of the participants in the festival also dress up in period costumes, which creates a unique and immersive experience for visitors.

Food and drink: There are plenty of food and drink stalls throughout the festival grounds, offering a variety of traditional Romanian dishes and drinks. Visitors can sample local specialties such as grilled meats, sausages, and cheese, as well as traditional Romanian desserts and pastries.The Sighisoara Medieval Festival is an exciting and unique event that offers visitors a glimpse into Romania's medieval past. The festival's combination of historical reenactments, traditional crafts and artisanal demonstrations, and delicious food and drink make it a must-see event for anyone visiting Romania.

The Sighisoara Medieval Festival Experience

On the first day I experienced the Sighisoara Medieval Festival of the Romanians, I felt like I had stepped back in time. As soon as I walked through the gates of the ancient citadel, I was greeted by the sights and sounds of a bygone era.

The streets were lined with vendors selling everything from hand-crafted pottery to traditional Romanian foods. Musicians played lutes and tambourines, and dancers twirled in colorful skirts and vests. The air was filled with the sweet aroma of roasting meats and the sharp tang of spices.

As I wandered through the crowds, I was mesmerized by the intricate costumes and ornate decorations on display. Knights in shining armor paraded through the streets on horseback, while jugglers and acrobats entertained the crowds with their feats of strength and agility.

In the evening, the main square was transformed into a medieval banquet hall, with long tables set up under a canopy of stars. We feasted on spit-roasted lamb, hearty stews, and fragrant breads, all washed down with copious amounts of locally brewed beer and wine.

As the night wore on, the festivities only grew more intense. Fire-eaters and sword-swallowers took to the stage, while jugglers performed death-defying stunts with flaming torches. Finally, as the sun began to rise over the ancient citadel walls, I stumbled back to my hotel room, exhausted but exhilarated from my first taste of the Sighisoara Medieval Festival.

Nightlife in Romania

Romania offers a vibrant and diverse nightlife scene that caters to all tastes and preferences. The country's major cities such as Bucharest, Cluj-Napoca, Timisoara, and Constanta, are home to a variety of entertainment options ranging from clubs, bars, pubs, and lounges to live music venues, theaters, and cultural events.

Bucharest, the capital city of Romania, is known for its lively and dynamic nightlife. The Old Town area, also called Lipscani, is a popular destination for tourists and locals alike, with its numerous bars, clubs, and pubs. The area is renowned for its vibrant and energetic atmosphere, with music and laughter filling the streets until the early hours of the morning.

Some of the most popular nightclubs in Bucharest include Control Club, Kristal Glam Club, and Bamboo.

Night view of Bucharest city in Romania.

Cluj-Napoca, a university town located in the northwest of Romania, is also famous for its nightlife. The city's streets are lined with a range of bars and pubs, catering to a young and diverse crowd. Some of the most popular nightclubs in Cluj-Napoca include Midi Club, Diesel Club, and Obsession Club.

Timisoara, located in the western part of Romania, is a vibrant and cosmopolitan city with a diverse nightlife scene. The city's main square is lined with cafes, bars, and restaurants, making it a popular destination for both locals and tourists. The city's nightlife is diverse and includes everything from jazz clubs and live music venues to techno clubs and underground parties.

Constanta, a seaside city located on the Black Sea coast, is also renowned for its nightlife. The city is home to a range of bars, clubs, and lounges, many of which are located on the beach, offering spectacular views of the sea. Some of the most popular nightclubs in Constanta include Fratelli Beach & Club, Ego Club, and La Mama Club.

In addition to the above-mentioned cities, Romania is also home to a range of cultural events and festivals that take place throughout the year, offering visitors a chance to experience the country's rich culture and heritage. Some of the most popular cultural events and festivals include the Transylvania International Film Festival, the George Enescu Festival, and the Medieval Festival in Sighisoara.

Romania's nightlife scene is vibrant and diverse, catering to all tastes and preferences. Whether you're looking for a quiet night out with friends or a wild party, Romania has something to offer.

I remember the night like it was yesterday. I was in Bucharest, Romania, and I had heard so much about the city's vibrant nightlife scene that I couldn't wait to experience it for myself. As soon as the sun set, I headed out into the city to explore.

I wandered through the winding streets of the Old Town, taking in the lively atmosphere and the sound of music and laughter that filled the air. The streets were crowded with people, all of whom seemed to be in high spirits and ready to party.

As I walked, I came across a club that caught my eye. The music coming from inside was loud and infectious, and I could feel my feet starting to tap along to the beat. Without hesitation, I made my way inside.

The club was packed with people, all of whom were dancing and having a great time. The music was a mix of Romanian pop and international hits, and the energy in the room was electric.

I ordered a drink from the bar and took a moment to take in my surroundings. The walls were covered in neon lights and the dance floor was packed with people moving to the rhythm of the music. I could feel the excitement building inside me, and I knew that this was going to be a night to remember.

As the night wore on, the crowd grew more and more energetic. People were dancing on the tables, drinks were flowing freely, and the music was getting louder and more intense.

Before I knew it, the sun was starting to rise and the club was starting to empty out. I stumbled out into the daylight, feeling exhilarated and alive. The experience had been everything I had hoped for and more, and I knew that I would never forget that night in Bucharest.

Practical information/rules and regulations about Romania and some detailed maps.

Here are some practical information for visitors traveling to Romania:

Currency: The official currency of Romania is the Romanian leu (RON). You can exchange foreign currency at banks, exchange offices, or ATMs.

Language: The official language of Romania is Romanian. English is widely spoken in major cities and tourist areas.

Climate: Romania has a temperate-continental climate, with four distinct seasons. Summers can be hot and humid, while winters can be cold and snowy.

Transportation: Romania has an extensive public transportation system, including buses, trams, and trolleybuses. Taxis are also widely available. If you plan to rent a car, be aware that driving can be challenging due to the poor condition of some roads and aggressive driving behavior.

Accommodation: Romania has a variety of accommodation options, including hotels, hostels, and apartments. Prices vary depending on the location and level of luxury.

Food: Romanian cuisine is diverse and flavorful, with influences from neighboring countries such as Hungary and Turkey. Popular dishes include sarmale (stuffed cabbage rolls), mici (grilled minced meat rolls), and ciorba (sour soup).

Safety: Romania is generally a safe country for visitors, but it is always advisable to take normal precautions, such as not leaving your valuables unattended and being aware of your surroundings.

Electricity: The voltage in Romania is 230 V, and the frequency is 50 Hz. The plugs are the European standard type C and type F.

Visas: Citizens of most EU countries, as well as some other countries, do not need a visa to enter Romania for up to 90 days. Check with the Romanian embassy in your home country to confirm if you need a visa.

Emergency numbers: The emergency number for police, fire, and ambulance services in Romania is 112.

Some important rules and regulations that visitors and tourists need to know about

Respect local laws and customs: Every destination has its unique laws, customs, and culture. Tourists should take the time to understand and respect them to avoid any cultural misunderstandings and legal issues.

Follow safety protocols: Visitors should be familiar with safety protocols in their destination and adhere to them, including traffic rules, safety guidelines, and emergency procedures.

Be mindful of the environment: Tourists should be mindful of the environment, avoid littering and pollution, and conserve resources such as water and electricity.

Dress appropriately: Visitors should dress appropriately according to the culture and customs of their destination, especially when visiting religious or historical sites.

Be respectful of locals: Tourists should be respectful of locals and avoid any behavior that may offend or disrespect them. This includes speaking in a respectful tone, avoiding taking photographs without permission, and not interfering in local customs and traditions.

Be cautious with your belongings: Visitors should be cautious with their belongings, including valuables and travel documents, and avoid leaving them unattended in public areas.

Observe health and hygiene protocols: Tourists should observe health and hygiene protocols, including vaccination requirements, mask-wearing, and social distancing measures, to avoid spreading diseases or contracting illnesses.

It is crucial to research the specific rules and regulations of the destination before traveling to ensure a safe and enjoyable experience.

Conclusion

In conclusion, Romania is a fascinating and diverse country that offers a wealth of cultural and natural attractions for travelers. From the stunning scenery of the Carpathian Mountains to the historic cities of Bucharest, Cluj-Napoca, and Brasov, there is something for everyone here. Visitors can enjoy delicious Romanian cuisine, sample local wines, explore medieval castles and fortresses, soak in the healing waters of spa resorts, and experience the warm hospitality of the Romanian people. Despite its turbulent past, Romania has emerged as a modern and vibrant country, full of vitality and potential. Whether you are looking for adventure, relaxation, or cultural immersion, Romania is a destination not to be missed.

UKRAINE
HUNGARY
Satu Mare
Baia Mare
Botosani
MOLDOVA
CHISINAU
Iasi
Oradea
Cluj-Napoca
Targu Mures
Bacau
Arad
ROMANIA
UKRAINE
Timisoara
Sibiu
Brasov
Galati
Braila
Buzau
Ploiesti
Pitesti
BELGRADE
BUCHAREST
Craiova
Constanta
SERBIA
BULGARIA

www.ingramcontent.com/pod-product-compliance
Ingram Content Group UK Ltd.
Pitfield, Milton Keynes, MK11 3LW, UK
UKHW022010190726
13853UKWH00004B/1859

9 798387 673399